milk and romance

by kiki kahn

Dedicated to all the singles who have ever laughed with
their friends about terrible dates.

Milk and Romance

Copyright © 2017 Kiki R.K. Kahn

All rights reserved.

First Printing: 2017.

Cover Design by Kiki Kahn

Illustrations by Kiki Kahn

ISBN-10: 1979895422
ISBN-13: 978-1979895422

contents

milk and romance

this book is inspired by (supposedly) true tales of little (and big) things people have done that made their dates think 'you are <u>not</u> the one.'

first
the weirdo

milk and romance

one guy asked me to milk his prostate.

i declined.

but i made the mistake of telling a friend about it.

the next time she saw him she shouted,

"prostate milk!"

i dated a man who took 10-second showers.

i asked why he was always so quick.

he said, **"i only wash my pooper, honey!"**

in his texan drawl.

he kept saying,

"arrrg! let the dog see the rabbit,"

in response to everything

from food to tits.

he told me

he wanted to attack me with his

heat-seeking **missile**.

on our first date he told me

it was too bad i'd be one of the first to die

when "the revolution comes"

the worst was **mr briefcase man**,

whose seduction routine was to extract a briefcase from under his bed like some kind of sex magician, and remove items one by one…

baby oil, ta dah!

condoms, ta dah!

he could only come by wanking himself. after a kiss and fumble he'd sprawl on the bed, briefcase at hand, masturbating furiously whilst staring at me. i wasn't allowed to 'interfere'.

afterwards he'd extract a baby wipe from the magic briefcase of sex to clean himself before enquiring if i had enjoyed it.

ermm.

i never could look at a briefcase the same way again.

he was completely obsessed

with wanting me to

dress up as a cat

at a bar my date
ordered himself a

pint of milk,

and was disapproving
when i ordered a

red wine.

he **mewed** during sex.

what a turn-off.

as he was cumming he'd frantically say,

"you're gonna make me make a mess"

or

"i'm gonna make a mess."

he seemed a catch.

kind, good looking, great car, popular.

except that he thought whispering
"penetration" in my ear was sexy.

uh. no.

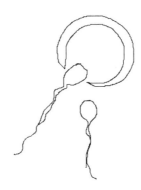

> *maybe penetration-man is a secret super-hero. he shoots webs from his nethers and swings from buildings, rescuing people.*

and then he whispers "penetration" in their ears until they swoon in delight.

Penetration

he reminded me of brad pitt. i thought he was perfect until i realized he said **"magic"** every time after sex.

he was no magician.

his "magic"-ing got a bit much, so i left.

> **what?!** *brad pitt could even whisper "penetration" at me and i wouldn't throw him out of bed! hell, i'd find it hot.*

> *depends:*

brad-pitt-a-like with voice like brad pitt purring "magic" into your ear: no problem.

brad-pitt-a-like with voice like the bedazzling swifty-mcgoo squeaking "magic!" every time after: hell no.

he began talking dirty during sex,

in a yoda voice.

after the first kiss one announced

he couldn't go any further as he was

"hung like a hamster"

why the feck would you describe it like that?!!!

on our first date he arrived with an **apple**

and held it up to my face like he was a disney witch,

quirked his eyebrow and purred in a slow (what he thought was seductive) voice,

"would you like a bite of my … … apple?"

no, i would not.

he tried to teach me how to dry myself after a shower.

in bed he seemed to think

i needed audio description

of what was happening.

he called his penis **private percy**.

he was silent during the deed.

it was creepy as fuck.

i couldn't tell when he had come.

i do like to know if they are enjoying themselves!

one night he made me listen to a rap song that he said

totally explained his feelings.

so i listened to the indecipherable lyrics,

while he gazed weirdly at me and beat his fist onto his chest.

the narcissist

apparently people were always telling him he had such a lovely smile,

so he would pull this fake cheesy grin during sex.

i gave him so many dirty looks

til he realized he'd be better off

saving it for the mirror.

he wouldn't drive as he "didn't see the point", but

he was always wanting rides

everywhere.

if he asks for a date on public transport he should have his train behavior observed first.

anyone who **manspreads** should be automatically rejected.

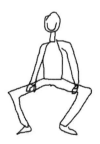

he was a one night stand at university

who kept whispering,

"no falling in love,"

in my ear mid-sex.

he believed he was a **disco god**

and would wriggle and jiggle

and do a pointy finger thing

on the dance floor.

mr-twice-my-age liked to growl at me that he was

"randy as a ram".

he was a complete caveman and was scarily ginormous downstairs, which he seemed to think made up for no technique and no foreplay.

it didn't.

during sex he'd shout, "you're not leaving this room until you have an orgasm."

i might have had to fake a few.

he was a **mr tiny penis** who thought he was god's gift and demanded,

> **"do you love it?** do you love it?" over and over during sex.

i thought it would hurt his feelings if i told him

> i couldn't feel it

> > let alone love it.

he had a mane of curly hair that he adored and considered to be one of his best 'features',

and his proud lopsided ape-walk made it **flop** about with every stride.

one day he bent down to **thrust** the top of his head at me and said, "oh, go on then!"

startled, i asked "what?!"

and he told me i was welcome to run my fingers through his hair.

i declined.

he thought he was irresistible. he wasn't.

he sang, "you just died in my arms tonight,"

whilst looking at me meaningfully.

i didn't know what to make of that

but mostly cringed.

he called himself the **'sperminator'**.

he was 5 foot 3, and was incredulous

when i declined his offer of a date.

mid-sex he declared he had **magic hands**.

looking really pleased with himself,

he proceeded to jiggle his fingers at me until i
faked an orgasm

just so he'd stop.

"told you so," he said,

with a self-satisfied smirk.

apparently his ex had said he had magic hands.

she created a monster.

he was a smug poker

who jabbed at me until

i faked it,

and then was so very pleased with himself.

he used to say,

  "there you go" as he came,

  like it was a gift for me.

no thanks.

he reminded me of a rock star i'd fancied,

so when he stood in front of me and performed his **'tree dance'**, by standing still while swaying his arms all over the place,

i didn't run screaming straight away.

i had sex with him and it was crap.

oh why did i not let myself be warned off by the tree dance?

a friend had a fling with a rampant lover.

the first time he came to her house he turned up with a big van full of his **vinyl collection** and persuaded her to store it because his girlfriend had chucked him out.

it is still has it in her garage some years later and she is getting mightily cheesed off!

whenever he said something he thought was funny or that i'd enjoy,

he would do this lop-sided smile, dip his head to look down and then slowly up

and flutter his eyelashes. i bet he practiced it in front of a mirror.

he must have thought it was sexy or cute or whatever.

  but actually he just looked like a prick.

> *was it like princess diana?*

i was middle-aged and found myself single.

a date talked about himself all evening, but i gave him the benefit of the doubt as i thought it was nerves.

the chemistry was there so we ended up doing the deed. he was quick and selfish, and then got uo straight afterwards to go home.

i was furious and told him why. his reply was, **"but I thought ladies didn't have orgasms."**

and this was a scientist for heavens sake!

the manchild

he lived at home with his mom but pretended she was his landlady.

she even went along with it.

he put on a baby voice which he thought was hilarious.

my ovaries shriveled at the sound.

cinder-fella

what a martyr

bought me gifts he couldn't afford,

so he could revel in his

'i'm shackled-to-a-mercenary-woman' act.

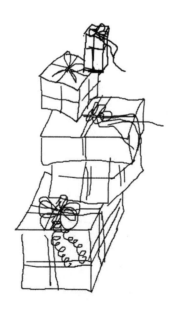

he used to get random erections (frequently in the frozen food section)

and thought it was fine to press it up against me

while groping my bum.

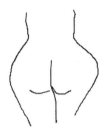

he used to squeeze my boobs in bed and say

"honk honk".

he'd come to hang out at mine and say things like,

"oh, i thought you said you were going to get me a drink,"

    when i'd said nothing of the sort.

this was his way of asking.

    if you want a fucking drink either help yourself or ask for one. don't make shit up.

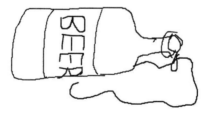

he was a short man who lied frequently

about his height to get dates.

he liked to do it against the washing machine on
its spin cycle as it would

'make it better for me.'

we ate at a nice restaurant, where he ordered frogs legs.

when he'd finished he proceeded to dance the little foggy leg bones across the table toward me,

whilst singing in a kermit voice.

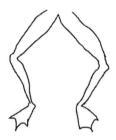

he said "mmmm" when he kissed me.

i once dated guy who referred

to his penis as his sword.

the unexpected

my sister was getting on well with a guy who she met online. after a few dates she invited him back to hers.

on the wall was a lovely family photo of us all, and she caught him looking curiously at it.

our dad had died a few years back so mum had been getting 'back on the wagon'.

it turned out my sister's new man had shagged our mum.

he called me "**hunny**" in a text message.

seeing it written down like that

gave me the rage.

he counted down to his orgasm from 5.

one told me on our first date that god had told him
i was his wife.

i've heard he's gay now.

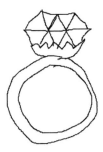

he had completely straight pubic hair.

it was so long!

i dumped someone once when they said they said they loved jean claude van damme films and bon jovi.

there was simply no point continuing.

i went on date with a weirdo because i loved his
long hair.

i soon discovered that he was just too tired to
get it cut,

along with his fingernails and toenails.

he was also too tired to eat,

or do anything in bed.

he slapped his own arse

and screamed **yes!**

as he came.

he shaved all the hair off his entire body and had
head-to-toe stubble.

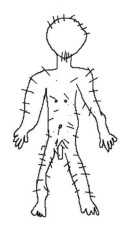

he had unrefined calves.

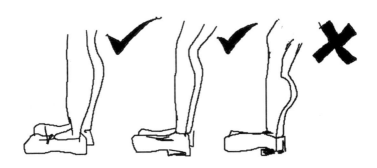

after a night out

he tore his shirt off at the top of my stairs

in manner of tarzan

and ripped the buttons off.

he said "pass me your pussy" during sex.

my friends all know i only date people with iphones... he didn't.

him: i like your sweater.

me: thanks.

him: what's it made from?

me: mohair

him: (silent for several minutes.)

him: (concerned face) but what about the poor mo's??

i hadn't realized there were so many pencil penises out there.

he had one long hair

growing out of his shoulder.

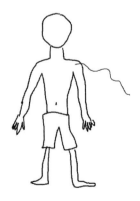

after visiting my house for the first time he informed me,

"we will get a good price for this once we are married."

i jokingly asked him if we'd live at his,

no, he replied. his parents, who lived in another country, were getting old and needed care

... so we would live with them.

the lad

he set fire to his fart.

date: "do you like cheese?"

me: ... "yes."

date: "well you'll love these," whilst gabbing his crotch.

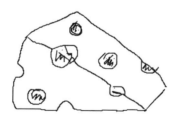

he got drunk and couldn't – ahem – perform,

and so spent the evening telling me in staggering detail of the marvelous life he'd have after getting rich and famous off the back of a great scheme he has.

but he can't tell me what it is or i might steal it.

he said **"sangwich"**

his constant farting and

asking someone to pull his finger

before he let one rip.

he said banter 10 times

in the first 20 minutes of meeting.

he said,

"you remind me of a carpet.

because I really want to lay you."

he was a public knife-licker.

one guy liked to refer to himself in the third person during sex.

stuff like,

     that's right, joe, just like that.

     she likes that, doesn't she, joe?

     pump harder, joe.

he was his own little cheering squad.

by the end i was thinking,

     oh just fuck off, joe.

the gentleman

my date took me to a lovely restaurant.

he turned up in a grandad jacket with leather elbow patches,

and proceeded to tear apart the coasters and fashion origami flowers from them.

presenting them to me one by one, he pronounced,

"these are for you, my lady."

one of the most annoying things about him was that he called herbal teas, herby tea.

as in, "do you want another herby tea?"

it irrationally wound me up.

he kept calling me his 'queen',

and made references to me

'sitting on his throne.'

i received a text from a guy that said,

"please send me a picture of your

mammary glands."

he treated his children like angels who could do no wrong,

and was scared to tell them off when they were being terrible.

thus making me into the **wicked step-mother**,

as i wouldn't tolerate any rudeness to me or my children.

he silently smiled at me

the whole way through sex,

only breaking the silence occasionally to say

"delicious".

he was a posh fella who

went to an all boys' school and

called his dogs his 'girlfriends'.

during the deed he gave me a running
commentary in strangely clinical terms,

but a **feverish** tone of voice:

> janice, i'm putting my penis into you!

> janice, i'm thrusting into you!

> janice, i'm ejaculating into you!

it was hilarious for all the wrong reasons.

> *> janice, was he perhaps a driving
instructor?*

he declared his bedroom a

'no clothes zone'.

and in the morning made me dress in the bathroom.

he also had a habit of saying,

"i just want to pleasure you m'dear,"

as a prelude to sex.

we lasted a month before i ran off screaming.

the deviant

he told me to keep my tights on

and then ripped a little entrance hole.

he tried repeatedly to sneak his penis in

without a condom.

in the middle of the night he got out of bed to visit the fridge.

i eventually discovered he was secretly banging his own arse with a carrot.

he was a low grade kleptomaniac.

i'd put something small down and he'd put it in his pocket.

he also got a kick out of lying about odd things

like where he was born.

one guy yelled out "heil hitler!" very loudly, and in my parents' house.

he rolled with laughter

while i clung to the duvet in shock.

he thought it would be hilarious as i'm jewish.

it was not.

i couldn't face my parents for months!

he liked to put his cock in a cage.

> *wtf is a cock cage?*

> *google is your friend.*

> *google is not my friend! i've been caught out before by tea bagging, and can't unsee these things! why would you put a cage on it???*

i was just about to have sex with a guy.

it was all building up nicely,

    and then he said,

        "i am sweating like a rapist."

the disgusting

he had claw feet and really long toenails.

and once accidentally scratched my leg with his toenail in bed.

yuck.

i briefly dated a guy who would get random erections at inopportune times.

we'd be walking down the street and he'd suddenly say,

"oops, there i go again."

i ill-advisedly had sex with a cameraman who
said,

"sorry, I'd have had a wank earlier if I'd known i
was going to pull."

the shock!

i avoid cameramen generally.

i have known many, and all have been

randy little minge-monkeys.

he would put his fingers to his bum when farting,

then would sniff his fingers.

his clothes always smelled of mildew,

and he put blankets on his windows instead of buying curtains.

he didn't brush his teeth the morning after our first
night together

and then kept trying to kiss me

with his death breath.

i caught him wiping his hands

on my kitchen curtains.

he breathed too loudly.

i'm not listening to that for the next 40 years,

goodbye.

that was a decade ago and i still get the occasional 'accidental' pic of his downstairs.

it stopped when i threatened to facebook the next one.

the unfortunate

i had fancied him for a year.

when we finally got together he made **exactly** the same noises as my

beloved little terrier

when it was humping a cushion.

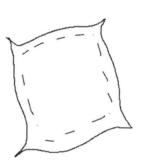

he had a giant head.

he looked like a caricature of himself.

the problem was how he looked when walking.

he kind of bounced.

he was really nice,

but i couldn't hack it.

i was at the chatting-on-the-phone stage with one guy, and he used the word "**chuckle**"

and that was the end of that.

he had an acorn willy.

i didn't know what to do with it.

he couldn't pronounce the word nuclear.

he said it like 'new killer'.

i can't fancy people with a big dimple in the chin (like john travolta).

i know it's not their fault but boy do i find it off-putting.

his jeans were too short.

his jeans were too high.

he said,

"hey ho, the wind and the rain,"

whenever he felt that there was a lull in the conversation.

the back of his head was irritatingly flat

and i had this awful desire to smack it.

so i ended it.

he brought me a 32 inch TV and about twenty other gifts on only our second date (near christmas).

sweet i suppose, but it freaked me out.

i dreamt he was a weirdo chasing me around grand central station.

he was perfectly nice,

but i couldn't forget the dream so

i had to dump him.

the mama's boy

he looked perplexed

about a woman in a picture having

underarm hair.

i hated his mom's tiny dogs.

mr oxford-educated lawyer had

20 pairs of waist-high white Y-fronts

drying out on his heaters the first time we went
back to his place.

it killed the mood dead for me.

he was overly proud of his parents' house and how expensive it was,

and thought it made him better than his friends.

when he stayed over at my parents' house,

he searched my brother and dad's wardrobes to borrow a belt

and refused to admit how weird that was.

he cried when Take That split up and refused to leave the house for days.

he shagged me while his mum was asleep in the next room and while wearing a pair of her tights with a hole cut out for his cock.

> *was his surname bates, first initial N??*

tighty-whities were a passion killer,

and so was the man wearing them, when he told
me all sexual activity had to be finished by 10pm,

as that was when he liked to go to sleep.

he was a ridiculously nice guy,

but i couldn't handle someone who saw the whole world

as rainbows and unicorn's farts.

he turned up to see me with an empty cake box.

he'd bought me a cake but got peckish on the bus so ate it.

even teenage me knew you don't eat a woman's bloody cake!

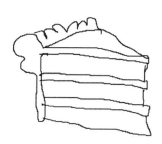

he cried because i didn't eat

all the broccoli he'd cooked for me.

he used the phrase

"wedding tackle".

half way through sex he started mumbling,

"oh no. these won't do."

and informed me

my nipples were the wrong color, and he
didn't like them.

afterwards he thoughtfully said that it was ok

as i could keep my bra on in future.

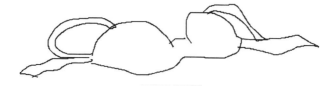

ABOUT THE AUTHOR

Thanks for reading my first book. I hope you had as much fun reading it as I had creating it. If so, please help a girl out and leave a review ☺ or recommend it to a friend you think will love it.

For news about future books join my mailing list (click here) or use the URL below:
http://bit.ly/2ziaQrC

Encourage me to tweet by following me here: @kahnbooks

Interior illustrations by Kiki Kahn
Cover design by Kiki Kahn

happy hunting

Made in the USA
Middletown, DE
14 December 2017